MW01157089

DATE DUE

Everything
You Need to
Know About

The Dangers of Computer Hacking

Computer hackers are often teenagers just like you.

Everything You Need to Know About

The Dangers of Computer Hacking

John Knittel and
Michael Soto

The Rosen Publishing Group, Inc.
New York

"Step up to red alert."
"Sir, are you absolutely sure? It would mean changing the bulb."
— *Red Dwarf*

To our parents for our first computers.
To Jennifer for turning off the TV and making us write this book.
To Jazz and Chaos for not sitting on the keyboard when we were trying
to finish.

The authors would like to thank the editors of the Jargon File 4.0.0 for creating such a useful reference. The Happy Hacker Web site also deserves our thanks for supplying us with many hours of entertainment. And finally we would like to give a special thanks to the members of 2600 and AntiOnline for providing us with such interesting reading over the years.

Published in 2000, 2003 by The Rosen Publishing Group, Inc.
29 East 21st Street, New York, NY 10010

Library of Congress Cataloging-in-Publication Data

Knittel, John, 1973.
Everything you need to know about the dangers of computer hacking/ John Knittel and Michael Soto.
   p. 23 cm. – (The need to know library)
Includes bibliographical references and index.
Summary: This book explains what computer hacking is, who does it, and just how dangerous it can be.
ISBN: 0-8239-3764-X
1. Computer crimes—United States. 2. Computer hackers—United States. 3. Internet (Computer network). [1.Computer crimes]
I. Soto, Michael. II. Title. III. Series.
364.16'8—dc21

Manufactured in the United States of America

Contents

Introduction

With the rise in popularity of the Internet, the media is filled with more and more reports of computer break-ins and dangerous situations caused by hackers. Because of the large number of these attacks and the media's interest in them, law enforcement now considers computer crime a top priority. At the same time, however, computer hacking is still largely misunderstood.

What Is Hacking?

In order to understand what hacking is, you need to know the difference between hacking and cracking. In the media, the term "hacker" is used to describe a person whose only goal is to attack other people's computers and cause them harm. This is not accurate. In reality, hackers are extremely talented people who use their abilities to

The Work of Hackers

There are many good hackers out there. Hackers designed and built the Internet. Xerox's Palo Alto Research Center was made up of hackers who created many of the early computer and interface designs we are familiar with today.

Many hackers are well known. For example, when Bill Gates started Microsoft, he was a hacker. The software he created made personal computers useful. He designed the first compilers that could be used on a PC. (A compiler is a tool that converts programs into a language the computer can understand.) Gates made it possible for useful software to be made and run on your home PC.

Two other hackers, Steve Jobs and Steve Wozniak, started a company called Apple Computer. The computers that Apple built were the first personal computers that anyone could buy and use. When Steve Wozniak built the Apple I computer, he was trying to impress fellow computer hobbyists. If they had not had such an interest in computers, the PCs that everyone loves to use today would probably not exist.

Today Steve Jobs is the head of a company called Pixar, which made the first fully computer-generated feature-length film, *Toy Story*. Steve Wozniak eventually retired from Apple Computer and now teaches fifth- to eighth-grade students how to use computers.

All three of these remarkable individuals were hackers. They did not spend their time breaking into computer systems and causing damage. They simply enjoyed pushing the limits of computer technology.

find innovative ways to change how computers work. They do this by writing new programs and building hardware that no one has thought of before. Hackers use their vast knowledge to better the computer industry.

At the same time, however, there are those who erase other people's files, steal credit card numbers, or vandalize Web pages. These people may be called hackers by the media, but they are known by people in the computer industry as crackers. They are not highly regarded by those in the computer industry.

So why does the media use the word "hacker" instead of "cracker"? This is mainly for two reasons. When stories are written for newspapers and television, they contain words that everyone is familiar with. Since the general public does not know the term "cracker," the media use the closest thing possible. In this case, the word they use is "hacker." The other main reason is that crackers, wanting to make themselves look better in the public eye, continue to call themselves hackers.

This misuse of terms causes even more confusion in the media when a "good" hacker does something noteworthy. Since the media use the term "hacker" for describing illegal computer break-ins, if a story has to be written about a "good" hacker, a term such as "computer expert" is used. For this reason, there is rarely a story that mentions a "good" hacker.

With all this confusion, people have created new names to clarify the situation. Many "good" hackers are referred to as white hats, whereas crackers are called dark hats. For the purposes of this book, we will generally call them hackers and malicious hackers or crackers.

Hacking and Cracking—Crossing the Line

Although there seems to be a clear difference between hacking and cracking, sometimes the line can become a little blurred. Hackers can get too curious. In their

Steve Jobs, a successful hacker, revolutionized personal computing with the launch of the Apple Macintosh computer.

search for knowledge, white hats sometimes get themselves into trouble. In 1988, a programmer named Robert Tappan Morris made just such a mistake. He was testing security flaws in two major Internet utilities, "sendmail" and "finger." He decided to write a program that would spread across computers utilizing those flaws, but he misjudged how fast it would spread. His program infected 10 percent of all the computers on the Internet, causing them to slow down and crash. The total damages were estimated at $96 million.

Teens are especially likely to find themselves in the gray area between white hat and dark hat. The Internet is a very complicated place, and if you know how only half of it works, you can make some very big mistakes. Also, it may seem fun and tempting to cause break-ins and mess around with other people's systems. However, rather than being clever and harmless, these maneuvers can land you in jail.

In 1998, the federal government convicted and prosecuted the first juvenile for computer crime. With these new policies in effect, it is important that teenagers know exactly how much trouble they can get themselves into with the power of computer technology in the new millennium. This book explains what hacking is, who does it, and just how dangerous it can be.

Chapter 1

A History of Hacking

Hacking has a long history—it started even before computers became popular. The earliest form of hacking involved telephones and was called phreaking.

Phreaking began in the early 1970s, when the workings of the phone system were a mystery to almost everyone except those who ran it. Most people simply took phones for granted. However, a few people tried to figure out just how phones worked. The most famous of these was John Draper. Using only a toy whistle from a box of cereal, he was able to take control of AT&T's entire telephone system. He soon became known as Captain Crunch.

Curiosity eventually led phreakers to become interested in the computers that ran phone systems. Those who changed their focus from telephones to computers later became known as hackers.

Most early computer break-ins came from company employees seeking financial gain or wanting to get revenge in personal disputes. Generally an employee would learn a feature of the computer system and exploit it. For example, in 1971, disgruntled employees at the Honeywell Corporation disabled the Metropolitan Life computer network for a month. In 1973, a teller at New York's Dime Savings Bank stole $1 million. Although these incidents are considered computer crime, it was not until the early eighties that cracking, breaking into computer networks that one had no prior relationship with, became widespread.

The release of the movie *War Games* (1983) gave many people their first look at hacker society. In this film, Matthew Broderick portrays a misunderstood teen who, while trying to play a few new video games, accidentally causes a nuclear scare. The movie introduced thousands of computer-savvy teens to a new and potentially dangerous outlet.

Since then, with the widespread availability of computer and network access, the number of teenagers who hack has increased dramatically. With the increase in computer attacks also came an increase in the media's coverage of these events. It wasn't long before hackers gained nationwide notoriety.

The movie War Games *with Matthew Broderick and Ally Sheedy was one of the first dealing with computer hacking.*

Methods Used by Hackers

Just how do these hackers get in? These are just some of a few simple methods that are used over and over again to gain access to a system. Whereas most are fairly technical, some of them do not even require a computer.

These methods are potentially disastrous for the hacker who uses them. But it is important for everyone to know about them because all computer users are at risk of being exploited.

Dumpster Hopping

Although not very glamorous, one method of finding information is through dumpster hopping. As the name implies, this involves rummaging through a company's trash for documents, memos, or anything else that might provide some insight into its internal computer system. This method can also provide employee names and phone numbers enabling hackers to call and ask for passwords.

Social Engineering

How does a hacker call and ask for passwords? No faithful employee would ever give an unauthorized user access to a company's system, would he? Well, by pretending to be a fellow employee or computer administrator, a hacker can make up a story and ask an employee for help: "We're having a little trouble with your computer account. Could you give me your password so that we can log in to correct the problem?" If the story is believable, many people will casually hand over their passwords without thinking twice.

Sometimes hackers do not even have to call. In the past, hackers have fooled people by e-mailing new technical support numbers throughout a company and then simply waiting for the employees to call with questions.

Password Hacking

Whenever a person logs into a computer system, his or her name and password are checked against a password file that is stored on the computer. This file contains acceptable usernames and their passwords in an encrypted (disguised) form. If the name and password

As many hackers have shown, finding someone's password or breaking into a company's private files doesn't take much more than a little hard work and some perseverance.

entered match a pair in the file, the user is accepted into the system. Otherwise he or she is locked out.

All a hacker has to do to gain entry to a system is find an acceptable match. One way is to repeatedly send usernames and passwords into a computer until a match is found. Although this could be done manually, a hacker will normally use a program that does this automatically. It might take days or months to find a match, but persistence will usually pay off in the long run.

If a hacker already has some sort of access to a computer system, there is another, much more effective method of password hacking. It involves running a program that looks at all of the usernames and passwords that are listed in the password file. The program compares the encrypted passwords with a dictionary of common words.

If a password matches a word in the dictionary, the hacker has a new username and password that can be used to log on to the system. For example, if someone in the computer system uses the password "apple," the hacker's program will be able to discover this, and hackers can use that person's account to gain access to the entire system. This is why some computer systems can require that a number be used as part of the password. For example, "Apple7" is a safe password because it does not appear in a dictionary.

Once a hacker has gained access to another person's account, he or she can easily jump to other computers, since most people tend to have the same password on all of the computers they use.

Trojan Horses

Trojan horses are programs that are left behind by hackers after they get into a computer system. These programs serve many different functions, from erasing important files to allowing the hacker to return anytime he or she wishes.

The greatest difficulty with Trojan horses is that hackers disguise them to look like ordinary programs.

A computer and a phone connection, even through a cellular phone, are all a skilled hacker needs to cause havoc.

Even if you find hackers on your computer system and remove their access, they could easily return using a Trojan horse.

E-Mail Snooping

E-mail snooping is the Internet equivalent of listening in on someone else's phone calls. When someone sends an e-mail, the text of the document is simply sent from computer to computer across the Internet until it arrives at the recipient's machine. Using some basic programs, a person can intercept and read these messages. All a hacker has to do is wait for someone to send his or her password to a friend.

War Dialers

Malicious hackers looking for computer systems to break into can use a war dialer. A war dialer is a program that calls a range of phone numbers looking for other computers. When it finds another computer, it notes the number and continues. Malicious hackers can then attempt to break into the computers that the program has found.

Although many of the methods used to break into computers might seem rather complicated, almost any hacker or cracker can perform them with ease. Mastering the techniques involved, however, takes a great deal of effort. Even more complicated is learning how and why these techniques work.

Chapter 2

Who Are Hackers?

Hackers rarely fit the nerd stereotype of wearing broken glasses and pocket protectors. Usually they are intelligent, individualistic people with highly curious minds. Hackers love to tinker with gadgets and figure out how things work.

Hackers generally have many interests other than computers; they often favor reading, solo sports such as cycling and hiking, and intellectual games such as chess. Their lack of interest in group activities seems to stem from a lack of social interaction. The many hours spent alone in front of computers tends to limit the amount of time spent with other people and therefore the development of social skills. Socializing via online forums and chat rooms can feel much safer than interacting with people face-to-face.

Working alone on a computer may make some people favor solo sports instead of group activities.

A Psychological Profile

What specifically leads a person to become a malicious hacker? To answer this we can turn to procedures used by law enforcement officials. When they have a crime to investigate, they like to know what kind of person they are looking for. They create a psychological profile, a group of characteristics shared by many of the people who commit certain similar crimes, to help them.

Some people have theorized psychological profiles that would help describe criminal hackers. At the 1999 RSA Data Security Conference and Expo, Canadian psychologist Marc Rogers gave a talk called "The Psychology of the Hacker." Rogers broke down the general term "hacker" into several subgroups: newbies, cyberpunks, coders, insiders, and cyberterrorists. Although his is just a theory, it can help you understand what makes malicious hackers do what they do.

The two groups that get the attention of the media and law enforcement most often are the newbies and cyberpunks, primarily because they are the ones who frequently get caught. The first group, newbies, consists of novice computer users with very limited skill. Newbies tend to get themselves into a lot of trouble because they don't really know what they are doing. When a newbie tries to break into a computer system, he or she frequently uses other people's programs to do so. Since the newbie doesn't understand how the program works, the results can be very unpredictable.

Newbies, who have limited computer skills, can very easily get into trouble with the law.

Cyberpunks have some programming knowledge and tend to know what they are doing when it comes to breaking computer security. Although they are not experts, they get caught less often than newbies.

The main difference between newbies and cyberpunks is their awareness about what they're doing. Newbies have almost no idea how computer systems work and tend to make mistakes when breaking into them. Cyberpunks, on the other hand, know what they are doing and usually get caught not because they make mistakes but because they brag about their exploits to others.

The third group, coders, write the programs used by newbies and cyberpunks. Coders have a lot of prestige in the hacker community because they have the most knowledge about the inner workings of computer systems and software. Newbies and cyberpunks aspire to achieve their skill level.

Seventy to eighty percent of all malicious computer break-ins are committed by insiders. These insiders usually consist of computer-literate, disgruntled former employees. Since they already have access to the computer systems, it is very easy for them to cause damage or to steal company secrets.

The most dangerous and least discussed group are professionals, or cyberterrorists. These people hack for profit. They are the most highly skilled group and are almost never mentioned in the media because they rarely get caught. Governments and corporations hire these computer professionals to sabotage computers and steal information from rivals. One of Marc Rogers's main concerns is that almost nothing is known about this group, and because of that, psychological profiles cannot be created for them.

One last group, which is less well defined, is of people called hacktivists. These are politically motivated malicious hackers who deface Web pages and computer systems to promote their political goals. Unfortunately, it is not always clear whether these are actual political groups

There are different kinds of hackers. Some are curious while others seek financial gain and others wish to embarrass governments, businesses, or individuals.

or cyberpunks covering up their true reasons for breaking into computers in the first place.

Hacker Profiles

The average hacker is a white, middle-class male who is twelve to twenty-eight years old. Even though hackers tend to perform poorly in school, they are often very intelligent and curious.

Many hackers have limited social skills; they feel isolated or insecure. As a result, they may turn to computers as a way to tune out of reality, especially if their reality is difficult. Teens who are abused or neglected may prefer to explore a world where they feel that they have more power or control. The anonymity of the Internet is very attractive to them—they can choose to be anyone they wish. Hackers may choose impressive online names, such as "Destroyer" or "Cyclone," to make up for feelings of low self-worth.

Some teens become so involved in the cyberworld that they can sit at a computer for days at a time. Although "computer addictive disorder" has been used as a defense at criminal trials, no medical connection has been made between being addicted to using a computer and committing computer crime.

Three Reasons for Hacking

Within the hacker profile that Marc Rogers developed are three reasons for committing computer crimes. The first is "internal": The entire purpose of the attack is for intellectual motives. Those who hack for this reason do it for the sheer pleasure and benefit of gaining new knowledge.

Another motive for breaking into computer systems is the hope of gaining something. These "external" reasons can include getting jobs or money for successful computer break-ins. This has been known to happen. Some companies have a policy of hiring hackers as security experts for their computer systems.

An interest in computers can become an addiction. Many enthusiasts build up home computer systems as complex as any corporation's.

"Vicarious" reasoning is the belief that by hacking into a computer system, a person can become famous. Many young people today see stories of hackers and wish that they could have the same kind of recognition. Some hackers have even been praised by their government for breaking into foreign computers.

Opinions about hackers vary widely. They can be seen either as saviors or monsters. Even though the hacking world is a diverse place, everyone in it has one thing in common: They can all get into trouble.

Famous Hackers

There have been many famous hackers. Most of them are well known because they broke the law and got caught. Some have been given long prison terms. Here are examples of two such people.

Justin Tanner Peterson

In 1991, a man named Justin Tanner Peterson, later known as Agent Steal, was arrested for possessing a stolen car. The investigation that followed showed that he was guilty of much more. It turned out that Peterson had been breaking into computer systems. He was indicted for gaining unauthorized access to computers and possessing stolen mail and credit card numbers. Peterson's record was sealed after the FBI and U.S. Attorney's Office asked for him to be released from jail in order to help conduct investigations of other hackers.

He remained under FBI supervision from September 1991 until October 1993. During this time, Peterson helped the FBI in cases involving two other famous hackers, Kevin Mitnick and Kevin Poulsen. When the case was reopened in 1993, Peterson faced up to forty years in jail and a $1.5 million fine. During a meeting with his lawyer and the U.S. attorney, Peterson was asked if he was still committing computer crimes, and he admitted that he was. In fact, he had broken into several federal computers and a credit card information bureau. After realizing his mistake, Peterson asked if he could take a small break. During the break he disappeared. He remained on the run for almost a year, until he was captured only two blocks away from the FBI's West Los Angeles office. In March 1995, Peterson pleaded guilty to creating an illegal $150,000 wire transfer at Heller Financial. He was given thirty-six months in prison and thirty-six months' supervised detention, and he was fined over $38,000 in restitution.

Kevin Poulsen

The case of Kevin Poulsen, known as Dark Dante, was the first time a hacker was charged with espionage. Like so many before him, Kevin started out as a phone phreak. At age thirteen, he was playing with the phone company's internal switching systems. His first arrest was for breaking into the government's Arpanet, which later became the Internet. Later in 1991, he was again arrested for tampering with Pacific Bell's phones.

After years of breaking into government and military computers, Poulsen was offered a job by the defense industry as a security consultant testing Pentagon computer systems. Unfortunately, it appears that protecting government secrets wasn't as interesting to him as stealing them, and Kevin Poulsen returned to his former ways. During his employment with the government, Kevin is alleged to have stolen classified military secrets, broken into military computers, stolen records regarding official FBI investigations, and even wiretapped phone calls of Hollywood actresses.

In November 1989, Kevin Poulsen was indicted for conspiracy, computer fraud, money laundering, and wiretapping. Faced with the possibility of thirty-seven years in jail, Kevin fled. While on the run, Poulsen pulled off one of the most famous stunts in hacker history.

Radio station KIIS-FM in Los Angeles had a simple contest. If you were caller number 102 after a certain song was played, you would win a brand-new $50,000 Porsche sports car. While thousands of faithful radio listeners were calling the station hoping to get lucky, Dark Dante hacked into Pacific Bell and took control of the radio station's phone lines. Only Kevin's phone was able to go through, and all other callers got a busy signal. The prize was his.

After seventeen months, the FBI finally caught up with Poulsen. While in custody, Kevin attempted to break into FBI computers to erase all of the evidence against him. Espionage charges were added to his indictment when stolen classified documents were found in a locker that Kevin had rented. Poulsen eventually pleaded guilty to computer fraud, money laundering, and obstruction of justice. On April 10, 1995, he was sentenced to fifty-one months in prison and fined over $56,000 in restitution to various radio stations that he had scammed. At the time it was the most severe sentence ever handed down for a computer crime.

Chapter 3

Cybercrime Crackdown

Until recently, hackers who broke the law received little more punishment than probation or a small fine that was a mere percentage of the financial damage they may have caused. However, as computers have become more and more important in our lives, the damage malicious hackers can do is often much greater and more costly. New laws have been passed to accompany the increase in cybercrimes. The result has been punishments that better fit the crimes hackers commit.

Many companies have been slow to upgrade computer security systems in response to the increase in cybercrime. Hackers are usually one step ahead of most computer security systems. And whether deliberate or accidental, computer break-ins have become so easy that little kids can—and have—done it.

Security in Cyberspace As E-Commerce Grows

In 1996, a survey was presented at the Senate hearing on "Security in Cyberspace." A small group of security firms was able to account for $800 million in losses worldwide. In that same year, the American Bar Association did a survey of 1,000 companies and discovered that 48 percent of them had lost money because of computer fraud. The damages ranged from $2 million to $10 million. With the dramatic increase in Internet commerce, this type of fraud can only get worse. According to the Forrester Group in Cambridge, Massachusetts, trade on the Internet will grow from $43 billion in 1998 to $1.3 trillion in 2003—9.4 percent of all business sales.

Easy Targets

Over the last few years, Internet usage has grown at a phenomenal rate. As a result, major companies, as well as government agencies and communications systems, depend on computers and the Internet to become part

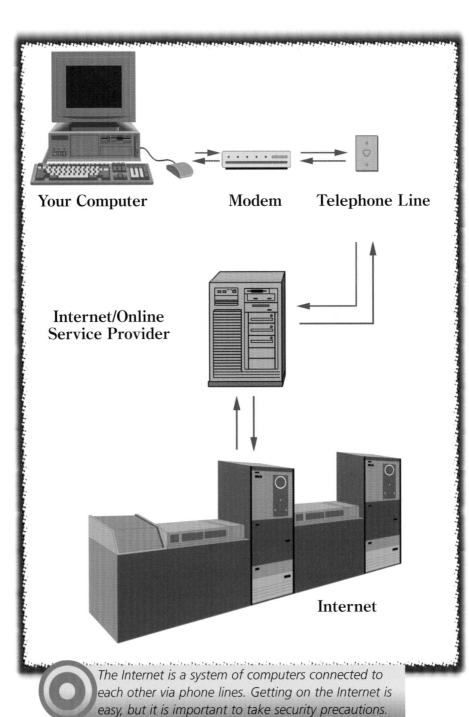

Your Computer Modem Telephone Line

Internet/Online
Service Provider

Internet

The Internet is a system of computers connected to
each other via phone lines. Getting on the Internet is
easy, but it is important to take security precautions.

of the global network. Unfortunately, many companies have been so eager to become a part of this network that they have set up their computer systems without taking proper security precautions. A company's employees often know little about the software on their computers. File-sharing, shared applications, and multiple computers downloading from a variety of Internet sources make accessing private files from outside the company extremely easy. Passwords and antivirus programs are no obstacle to a hacker. Furthermore, the new Internet businesses constantly need new software programs, which puts these businesses at risk because of the ongoing installation of new files.

In 2001, the FBI caught a highly organized ring of hackers who had stolen more than one million credit card numbers from the Web sites of over forty American businesses. The attacks, which came from Russia and the Ukraine, were incredibly simple. The hackers entered computers using a flaw in a Microsoft operating system, which allowed unauthorized users to disable security measures, access files, and even crash computers. People had known about the flaw since 1998. Microsoft had even issued public warnings and offered free, downloadable security "patches." Nonetheless, many companies didn't pay attention to the warnings. As a result, hundreds of thousands of dollars of damage occurred.

It can be very difficult to measure the damage a hacker does. A 2001 survey conducted by the Computer Security Institute (CSI) in conjunction with the San Francisco FBI's Computer Intrusion Squad, revealed that 85 percent of the large companies and government agencies that responded had been victims of computer break-ins during the previous year. Though 64 percent of the respondents suffered financial loss, only 35 percent knew the dollar amount. In fact, according to the FBI's National Computer Crimes Squad, between 85 and 97 percent of computer break-ins are not even detected. Despite this, it is estimated that, in 2000, $1.6 trillion in damage was caused by computer crime worldwide.

There are many ways malicious hackers can damage a company's computer system. The most popular is by stealing information, also known as industrial espionage. It is actually quite common for companies and even countries to hire hackers in order to steal important company or military secrets. Not only is this illegal, but it can lead to huge financial losses for corporations and put national security at risk.

Hackers and the Law

Cybercrime is such a new phenomenon that it has been tough not only to catch malicious hackers but also to decide how to punish them. Most laws regarding cybercrime are very new and still quite vague. With malicious hackers constantly accessing computers in new ways, it is often difficult for judges and juries— many of whom are not computer experts—to make informed decisions. Criminal defense attorney Jennifer Granick is well known for defending hackers accused of illegal activities. She recalls a preliminary hearing in which a witness talked about "cutting and pasting" text from one file to another. The judge responded: "You mean with scissors?" Defense attorneys like Granick worry that judges' lack of knowledge could lead them to give sentences that are overly severe. However, many judges are taking computer and technology courses to better understand these cases.

Another confusing problem the legal system faces is that so many offenders are minors. Historically, most federal crimes revolved around large sums of money, violence, or drugs. They didn't involve computers, and the criminals usually weren't juveniles.

The FBI knows that most hackers are kids who aren't particularly dangerous. More often than not they are well educated, upper-middle-class male teens with lots of time on their hands. Because of this, most juveniles convicted of computer crimes by federal courts receive light sentences. The most usual punishment is a probation period during which the hacker is prohibited from using a computer. However, with the rising incidence of computer crime, there has been a movement to increase sentences and to begin prosecuting underage malicious hackers as if they were adult criminals.

Meanwhile, new laws are being passed to tighten some of the many loopholes that hackers slip through. One example is the No Electronic Theft Act. It was passed in 1997 after an MIT student, David M. LaMacchia, set up an electronic bulletin board for distributing pirated software. Because the year of the crime was 1994, by law, LaMacchia couldn't be prosecuted for copyright infringement because he did not profit from his acts. Now, however, with the passage of this act, anyone who gives away software illegally can be prosecuted, even if he or she does not profit from it.

In 1996, President Bill Clinton signed the U.S. Economic Espionage Act. The act made it a federal crime to take, download, or possess trade secret information without the owner's permission. This means that anytime a hacker breaks into a computer system and looks at any private company information, even by accident, he or she is breaking the law.

Since then, the federal government has continued to make its fight against cybercrime and cyberterrorism a major priority. In 1998, the Department of Justice and the FBI created the National Infrastructure Protection Center (NIPC), which is made up of government agencies and private companies that work together to crack down on cybercrime and to ensure cybersecurity. The Department of Justice has also been hiring many attorneys and specialists in computer crime. At the time of the writing of this book, President George W. Bush was planning to announce a massive, nationwide cybersecurity "strategy" as well. The "strategy" will likely offer incentives to companies that beef up their security systems.

Hackers Who Got Caught

Because of their daring exploits and the subsequent media attention they attracted, many hackers have become celebrities. Following are case studies in which these hackers got caught.

Phiber Optik

Mark Abene first became interested in computers while hanging out in the electronics section of the A&S department store where his mother worked in Queens, New York. By the time he was twenty-one, he was better known as Phiber Optik, and he had become the digital world's first full-fledged outlaw hero. He grew to fame after being indicted on federal charges of unauthorized access to phone company computers and conspiracy to commit further computer crimes. The phone company claimed that Abene had used its computers to access credit bureaus, other computer systems, and to make free long-distance calls.

To make an example of him, in 1992, a Pennsylvania judge sentenced Abene to a year and a day in jail (without computer access) followed by three years' probation and 600 hours of community service. This was a harsh sentence at the time, and upon his release from prison, hundreds of sympathizers attended a "Welcome Home" party for Abene at a chic Manhattan club. Shortly after, *New York* magazine included him in their list of "100 Smartest People."

Analyzer

In February 1998, FBI agents raided the homes of two teenage boys in Cloverdale, California. The two boys, known online as Makaveli and TooShort, had taken part in one of the largest computer attacks the Pentagon had ever faced. They were not formally arrested, but their computers were confiscated. The two youths were eventually placed on probation.

It was soon discovered that their leader was an eighteen-year-old living in Israel named Ehud Tenebaum. Known as the Analyzer, he had been teaching the two youths how to get past complex security systems like those used by the government.

The attack included a computer system at NASA, seven U.S. Air Force sites, and four U.S. Navy sites. John Hamre, the former U.S. deputy secretary of defense, called it "the most organized and systematic attack the Pentagon [had] seen to date."

In Israel, Tenebaum gained celebrity status after being called "damn good" by Prime Minister Benjamin Netanyahu. A week later, he was used in a full-page

Ehud Tenebaum, also known as the Analyzer, has been charged in Israel with conspiracy and harming computer systems.

computer advertisement in Israel's largest newspaper, *Yedioth Ahronoth*. Tenebaum was placed under house arrest in Israel and questioned by local authorities.

Then U.S. Attorney General Janet Reno stated, "This arrest should send a message to would-be computer hackers all over the world that the United States will treat computer intrusions as serious crimes. We will work around the world and in the depths of cyberspace to investigate and prosecute those who attack computer networks." Tenebaum has been charged in Israel with conspiracy and harming computer systems.

Justin Boucher

Many times the dangers of hacking are not limited to being prosecuted in a court of law. For Justin Boucher, a senior attending Greenfield High School in Milwaukee, Wisconsin, it resulted in expulsion from school.

In fact, there is no proof that Justin did any hacking at all. At the end of his junior year, Justin wrote for an underground newspaper called *The Last*. Under a pen name, he wrote an article about hacking. The article, titled, "So You Want to Be a Hacker?" outlined methods to break the security of the school's computers.

When school officials found out that Boucher had written the article, they immediately brought it to the attention of the school board. The school board voted unanimously to expel Boucher for fourteen months.

Boucher's family, along with the ACLU, sued the school, claiming that it was violating his First Amendment right to free speech. An injunction was issued in September 1997 to allow Boucher to attend classes while the suit was being resolved. On January 9, 1998, however, the Seventh Circuit Court of Appeals stated that the injunction "jeopardized [the school's] authority to control disruptive students" and ruled in favor of the high school.

Kevin Mitnick

Kevin Mitnick is by far the most famous hacker of all time. Descriptions of Mitnick range from "cyberhero" "computer terrorist," depending on whom you ask. Several books have been written about his exploits, and a movie is in the works as well. He has spent more time in jail for computer crime than any other person.

Kevin Mitnick's earliest hacking exploit was breaking into his high school's administrative system. He didn't change any of his grades—he just wanted to see if he could do it. In 1981, Mitnick was arrested for stealing computer manuals from a Pacific Bell phone company switching station. Because he was seventeen, he was given only probation.

In 1982, Mitnick, in violation of his probation, was caught hacking computers at the University of Southern California (USC), where he wasn't even enrolled. He served six months at the California Youth Authority's Karl Holton Training School.

While at USC, he was reported to have broken into computer systems at NORAD, the North American Air Defense Command in Colorado. It was also believed that Mitnick seized control of phone company systems in New York and California. He was never officially charged for these alleged activities.

Next, Mitnick illegally accessed a computer called Dockmaster, the National Security Agency's gateway to the Internet. To gain access, he phoned a legitimate user and posed as a technician. By claiming that he was issuing new passwords, Mitnick was able to obtain the user's ID and password.

At age twenty-five, Mitnick was caught hacking into computers at MCI and Digital Equipment. He was accused of causing $4 million worth of damage to computer operations and stealing $1 million worth of software. Mitnick was convicted and given a one-year jail sentence to be served at a minimum-security prison in Lompoc, California. He was ordered not to touch a computer or modem. Upon his release, Mitnick was required to spend a year at a residential treatment program, where he took part in a twelve-step program designed to rid him of "computer addiction." Then, in 1992, after federal agents came to question him for possible parole violations, he disappeared.

In 1993, California state police issued another warrant for Mitnick's arrest. This time he was accused of wiretapping calls from the FBI to the California DMV.

He was supposedly using the information to gain illegal entry to the driver's license database.

On Christmas Day 1994, Mitnick, at the age of thirty, allegedly broke into a computer owned by Tsutomu Shimomura. Shimomura, an expert at computer security, began to track Mitnick. He was arrested in February 1995. Twenty-five thousand stolen credit card numbers were found on his computer.

This proved to be the most controversial hacker case of all time. In 1996, Mitnick pleaded guilty to a federal charge of cellular phone fraud and admitted to violating probation. The next year he was sentenced to two years in prison. He was still awaiting trial for twenty-five other counts of computer and wire fraud, possessing unlawful access devices, and intercepting electronic messages at that time.

Because of Mitnick's extremely long incarceration, and suspicion that he was set up, hacker groups began protesting, and the "Free Kevin" movement began in cyberspace. The protests included a legal defense fund that sold bumper stickers and asked citizens to write to government officials. There is also a Web site devoted to the fund at http://www.freekevin.com.

Hacktivists were known to change Web pages in protest for Kevin. The most famous of these activities was in 1997 when a group that called themselves PANTS/HAGIS broke into the Web site Yahoo!, the busiest Web site on the Internet. They changed the site to say that they had planted a virus and that anyone who visited the site would be infected. Supposedly, the virus was set to go off on Christmas Day if Mitnick was not freed. As it turned out, the virus did not exist.

On March 26, 1999, Mitnick accepted a plea agreement that required him to serve a total sentence of sixty-eight months. Formal sentencing was held on August 9, 1999. He was given a forty-six-month sentence and was ordered to pay $4,125 in restitution. In addition, he is not allowed to touch a computer or cellular phone without written permission from his probation officer.

Hacking Is No Laughing Matter

The previous cases show how serious the consequences can be for malicious hacking. Even when the intent is not malicious or when the damage done is minimal, punishments are increasingly severe. And it doesn't matter how old you are. Increasingly, courts are beginning to treat minor offenders as they would adults and punish them accordingly. Knowing what systems you're dealing with at all times and being aware of the consequences are key to becoming a "good" hacker.

Chapter 4

Becoming a "Good" Hacker

In order to become a "good" hacker, you must first understand how computers and software operate. Computers and software are complex and sophisticated tools. It can take years of learning and experimenting to master them and understand their capabilities.

Getting to Know Your Computer

Computers and software programs are constantly changing. New features, programs, and upgrades are introduced every day. Even after you become an expert, you'll have to spend a lot of time just staying up-to-date with the latest tools and developments. Of course, this fast-changing world is what makes hacking so exciting and such a challenge.

Becoming a computer whiz isn't easy—you have to master all aspects of your computer and gain a thorough knowledge of how networks function.

To be a "good" hacker, you have to get to know your computer better than you know the back of your hand. This means sitting down and spending time checking out all the programs installed on your computer. It also means getting to know your hardware and its components, which range from your hard drive to your modem. What do they do? How do they work? What happens if they stop working? If something does go wrong with your computer, try to fix it yourself before you call technical support. There are many Web sites that offer explanations on how to fix most problems. Soon you'll get so good you won't need to consult them.

Once you feel familiar with the computer itself and the programs installed on it, you can move on to learning how to write your own programs. Writing your own programs is what separates amateurs from bona fide hackers.

There are countless ways to program a computer. The most basic type of program to write is a script. Scripting languages, or programs, such as Perl, JavaScript, and AppleScript, tell other programs to perform certain functions in a specific order. Scripts are often used in Web pages. You can, for example, use a script to automatically count the number of users that visit your site or to change text and photos at a certain time of the day.

High-level programming languages, such as Java or C, allow programmers to create their own applications. First, the programmer writes an elaborately coded list, giving a computer instructions on how to perform a task. This code has to be converted from the alphabet we understand to the language of zeros and ones that a computer understands. This is done using a program called a compiler that creates the finished program you can run on your computer.

Having mastered your own computer, you can move onto learning how to communicate with other computers. A computer network consists of various machines that are linked together in order to share information with each other. The Internet is the world's biggest computer network, reaching nearly every part of the globe. Learning about connections and protocols and writing the programs that allow them to work together can open up the whole world to you, literally.

Security measures are necessary to keep outsiders from entering your computer and accessing your personal files. Security precautions include devising programs such as firewalls and passwords that keep intruders out.

Another security measure is encryption. Encryption transforms information into a mathematics-based code that cannot be read by anyone other than the person for whom it is meant. If you send an encrypted e-mail for example, the person who receives it can read it only if he or she knows the right password. Anyone else who tries to intercept the message will just see a mess of letters.

Learning How to Hack

Learning how to be a good and responsible hacker is fairly easy thanks to the many resources available on the Internet. Simply start by looking for sites about hacking on your favorite search engine. Sites that deal with computer programs and computer security can also be useful.

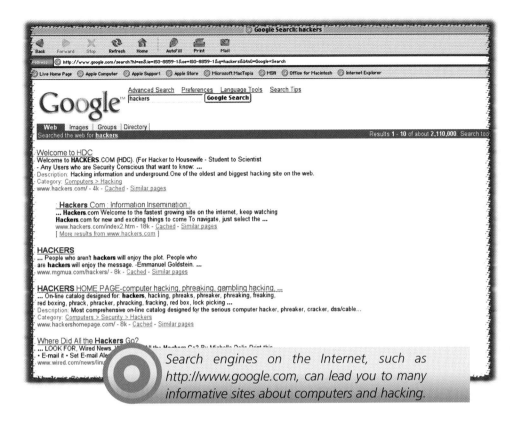

Search engines on the Internet, such as http://www.google.com, can lead you to many informative sites about computers and hacking.

One good Web site is http://www.antionline.com. It is for people who are fed up with having their computer systems broken into by malicious hackers and want to fight back. Maintained by security experts who keep track of all the new security problems, it offers tips on everything from how to choose a good password to how to find a job as a hacker.

San Francisco–based Computer Security Institute (CSI) is an organization that covers different aspects of computer and network security. Its Web site at http://www.gocsi.com offers a lot of information ranging from articles and surveys to postings about workshops and training seminars. Meanwhile, one of the best sites to learn more about encryption is RSA Data Security's site at http://www.rsasecurity.com.

Although the Web is a valuable tool, there are also many useful books available at your local library or bookstore. Some are listed in the For Further Reading section at the end of this book. These books cover a wide range of topics.

Being Responsible

As we saw earlier, even hackers who mean no harm can accidentally end up breaking the law and being punished. This occurs when inexperienced hackers start fooling around with systems and programs that they don't completely understand. They might not mean to cause damage, such as wiping out files or passing along a virus, but the damage is done, and unfortunately there is a price to pay.

Sending a virus by e-mail is illegal. So is breaking into a computer without permission. Even if you simply enter someone else's computer, you are breaking the law. Meanwhile, there are some places on the Web that actually do give you permission to break in. The addresses of some are given in the back of this book.

Ultimately, being a "good" hacker is all about behaving responsibly and considering the consequences of

There are many books and other materials available on computers and the pros and cons of hacking.

Hackers and Cyberculture

No one person can learn every aspect of a computer system. It takes hundreds of engineers and programmers just to make a system. So the computer community has come up with many ways of sharing information and know-how.

Before the Internet, computer enthusiasts communicated via modems and phone lines. They would contact a central computer called a BBS, which stands for "bulletin board system." Messages could be left there for others to read, covering every topic from music to computer programming. Other people could read the messages and reply with their opinions. Hackers could post messages asking others for help or bragging how they had just fixed a bug in some software. This way they kept in touch with their peers.

Today, Internet news groups have virtually replaced bulletin board systems. They are almost exactly the same except that many more people have access to these messages, and the information can be sent automatically to your computer.

Online chat rooms and Internet Relay Chat (IRC) are also popular forums. These can be thought of as computer party lines. Many people meet to talk about whatever they want to. Unlike a news group, a chat room is a live conversation. When you type something, your friends see it immediately and can type a message back to you. Chat rooms are the perfect meeting place for small groups of hackers discussing the day's events.

Now and then, people like to meet in person. Some hacker organizations hold monthly meetings all around the country. The most famous of these meetings is held by a group called 2600. Members gather in malls and other public places to discuss what they are doing and meet other people who are interested in computers and hacking.

Hackers also hold conventions. One of the most popular is called Def Con and is held once a year in Las Vegas. People from all over the world gather together to discuss computer security and other hacker issues. Many lectures are given, and companies set up booths to show off their software. This is a great place for people to exchange information and to be exposed to ideas that may not be covered at their local meetings.

All of these methods are used to communicate information. The information can vary from a new type of encryption that will make the Internet safer to a combination lock that can be broken into in a few minutes. Although a company might not want it known that its locks are unsafe, the hacker community sees it as a benefit to society to make these problems known. They do not promote exploiting this information for illegal purposes.

Many people say that it makes more sense just to call a company and explain that its product has a security problem. Unfortunately, most companies do not correct problems until they have become publicly known. Magazines such as *2600: The Hacker's Quarterly* have brought many potentially disastrous problems into the public eye so that they could be fixed before they were exploited.

your actions. As our lives become more and more dependent on computers and the Internet, hackers will play a more important role in society. Being a "good" hacker can lead to a challenging and high-paying job. Being a malicious hacker can lead to a prison sentence. The kind of hacker you become is up to you.

Glossary

BBS (bulletin board system) A computer that people call using a modem. After calling the computer, a person can post messages to other people and read recent news.

bug A mistake in a computer program.

chat room A place on the Internet where you can talk to other people by typing in messages.

compiler A program that converts programming languages into a form that a computer can understand.

cracker A person who illegally breaks into other people's computers.

data Information in a computer.

database An organization of information in a computer that can be easily searched and sorted.

download To transmit a file from another computer to your computer.

e-commerce The buying and selling of goods on the Internet.

e-mail Electronic mail is a message that can be sent across a network.

encryption The method of converting data into a form that cannot be read by others.

hacker A person who uses his or her skills to find new and innovative solutions to computer problems.

IRC Internet Relay Chat is a popular system for chatting with others on the Internet.

mail server A server that delivers and receives e-mail.

modem A device that allows computers to talk to each other over a phone line. It stands for "modulator/demodulator."

network A system of interconnected computers that can communicate with each other.

newsgroup A forum in which different subjects are discussed on the Internet.

news server A server that delivers and receives news.

password A secret code word that, when combined with a username, allows access to a computer.

phreaking The art of breaking into telephone networks illegally.

program A set of instructions for a computer that accomplishes a certain task.

programmer A person who writes programs.

server   A computer that provides services,
such as e-mail and news, to other computers
on a network.

software   A generic term for programs that are
used on computers.

switching station   What telephone companies use
to route phone calls.

Trojan horse   A malicious program that is disguised
to look like a seemingly harmless one.

username   An identifier that, when combined with
the correct password, allows access to a computer.

virus   A malicious piece of software that inserts
itself into other programs on a computer.

war dialer   A computer program that uses a modem
to call a series of phone numbers looking for other
computers.

Web server   A server that allows people to see
Web pages.

For More Information

U.S Department of Justice
Criminal Division, (Computer Crime and Intellectual
    Property Section)
10th and Constitution Avenue, NW
Washington DC 20530
(202) 514-1026
Web site: http://www.cybercrime.gov

National Cybercrime Training Partnership (NCTP)
National White Collar Crime Center
1000 Technology Drive, Suite 2130
Fairmont, WV 26554
(304) 366-9094
Web site: http://www.nctp.org/

Web Sites

Due to the changing nature of Internet links, the Rosen
Publishing Group, Inc., has developed an online list of
Web sites related to the subject of this book. This site is
updated regularly. Please use this link to access the list:

http://www.rosenlinks.com/ntk/coha/

For Further Reading

Books

Cringely, Robert. *Accidental Empires: How the Boys of Silicon Valley Made Their Millions, Battle Foreign Competition, and Still Can't Get a Date*. New York: HarperCollins, 1993.

Hafner, Katie, and John Markoff. *Cyberpunk: Outlaws and Hackers on the Computer Frontier*. New York: Simon & Schuster, 1991.

Littman, Jonathan. *The Watchman: The Twisted Life and Crimes of Kevin Poulsen*. New York: Little, Brown & Co., 1997.

Weigant, Chris. *Careers in Cyberspace*. New York: The Rosen Publishing Group, Inc., 1997.

Technical Reading

Kernighan, Brian, and Dennis Ritchie. *The C Programming Language*. Toronto, ON: Prentice Hall, 1988.

Schneier, Bruce. *Applied Cryptography*. New York: John Wiley & Sons, 1996.

Index

About the Author

Michael Soto is a programmer for a financial corporation in New York City. He is a graduate of the Cooper Union for the Advancement of Science and Art. To the best of his knowledge, he has no other notable accomplishments.

John Knittel is the manager of information systems for a publishing company in New York. He is a graduate of the Cooper Union for the Advancement of Science and Art. His interests are reading and cycling. He has never kissed a girl.

Photo Credits

Cover by Thaddeus Harden; pp. 2, 16, 25, 48 by Maura B. McConnell; pp. 10, 41 © Hulton/Archive/Getty Images; p. 14 © The Everett Collection; p. 18 © AP/Wide World Photos; p. 21 by John Bentham; p. 23 © Bachman/Uniphoto Picture Agency; pp. 27, 53 by Thaddeus Harden; p. 34 by Annie O' Donnell; p. 51 © google.com.

Series Design

Tom Forget

Layout

Tahara Hasan